ATTACK
OF THE...

FOUL FUNGI

By William Anthony

Enslow
PUBLISHING

Published in 2021 by Enslow Publishing, LLC
101 W. 23rd Street, Suite 240,
New York, NY 10011

Cataloging-in-Publication Data

Names: Anthony, William.
Title: Foul fungi / William Anthony.
Description: New York : Enslow Publishing, 2021. | Series: Attack of the... | Includes
glossary and index.
Identifiers: ISBN 9781978519954 (pbk.) | ISBN 9781978519978 (library bound) | ISBN
9781978519961 (6 pack)
Subjects: LCSH: Fungi--Juvenile literature.
Classification: LCC QK603.5 A584 2020 | DDC 579.5--dc23

CPSIA compliance information: Batch #BS20ENS: For further information contact Enslow Publishing, New York, New York at 1-800-542-2595

PHOTO CREDITS

All images courtesy of Shutterstock. With thanks to Getty Images, Thinkstock Photo and iStockphoto.

Used throughout (including cover) – chekart (background), Sonechko57 (slime), VectorShow (microbe characters), Alena Ohneva (vector microbes), Olga_C (circle image frame). Used throughout (excluding cover) – Photo Melon (clipboard), Lorelyn Medina (scientist characters). P4–5 – Prostock-studio, Rost9, p6–7 – XeKayeM, Sergey Fedoskin, p8–9 – Gamzova Olga, Piyada Jaiaree, p10–11 – chaipanya, Kateryna Kon, p12–13 – Kateryna Kon, BlueRingMedia, photo one, p14–15 – Hyde Peranitti, p16–17 – Kateryna Kon, moj0j0, p18–19 – lmfoto, Stu's Images (Wikimedia), p20–21 Kateryna Kon, sriulk, p22–23 – ede, Kateryna Kon, Natthawon Chaosakun

CONTENTS

Words that look like <u>this</u> can be found in the glossary on page 24.

TRICKY WORDS

FUNGUS = singular (one fungus)
FUNGI = plural (many fungi)
FUNGAL = having to do with a fungus or many fungi

BAD THINGS COME IN SMALL PACKAGES

Imagine the smallest thing you can. Now try to imagine something that's so small that you can't even see it. This is how small microorganisms are.

"Micro" means tiny. "Organism" means a living thing.

ARGH!

Get the <u>microscope</u>! We need to look at these things more closely.

Microorganisms are sometimes called microbes, and they are everywhere. They're on the ground, in the air, and in our water. They're even on our skin and inside our bodies.

FOUL FUNGI

Fungi are a type of microbe. They are alive and some are too small to see. Some fungi are much bigger, such as toadstools.

Fungi can grow that big?
We're doomed!

Fungi cannot make their own food. Instead, they break down dead plants and animals or feed off living ones.

"That poor tree. The fungi are taking over!"

Some fungi can be good. Yeast is a fungus that we use to make our bread rise. Other fungi live safely in our bodies.

"The bread is okay, people.
The bread is okay!"

Other fungi are not so good for us. Some can make us itch, give us rashes, and even be <u>poisonous</u> to eat.

FUNGAL INFECTION

"The fungi <u>invasion</u> has begun. We need to find out more!"

ATHLETE'S FOOT

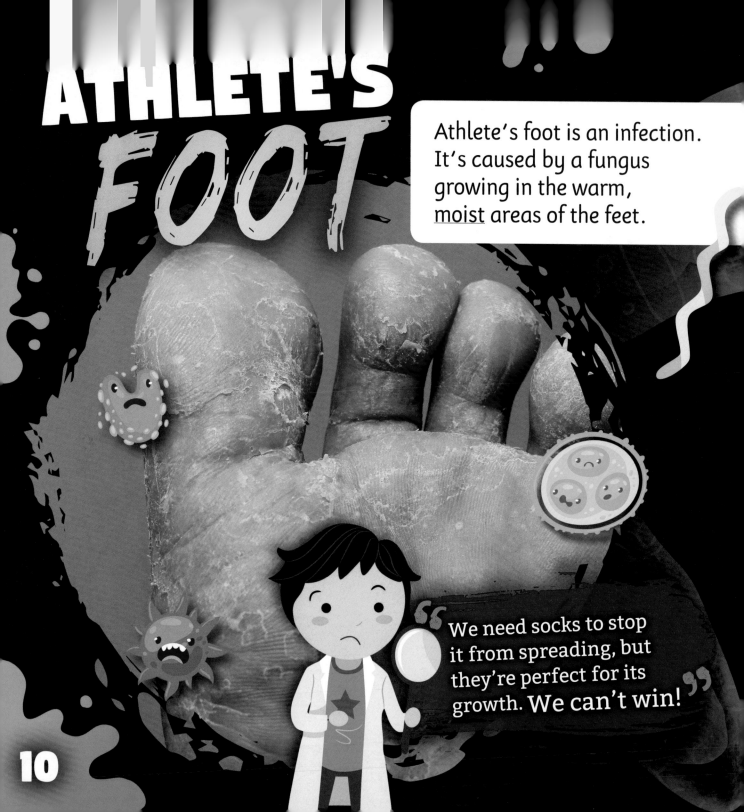

Athlete's foot is an infection. It's caused by a fungus growing in the warm, <u>moist</u> areas of the feet.

We need socks to stop it from spreading, but they're perfect for its growth. We can't win!

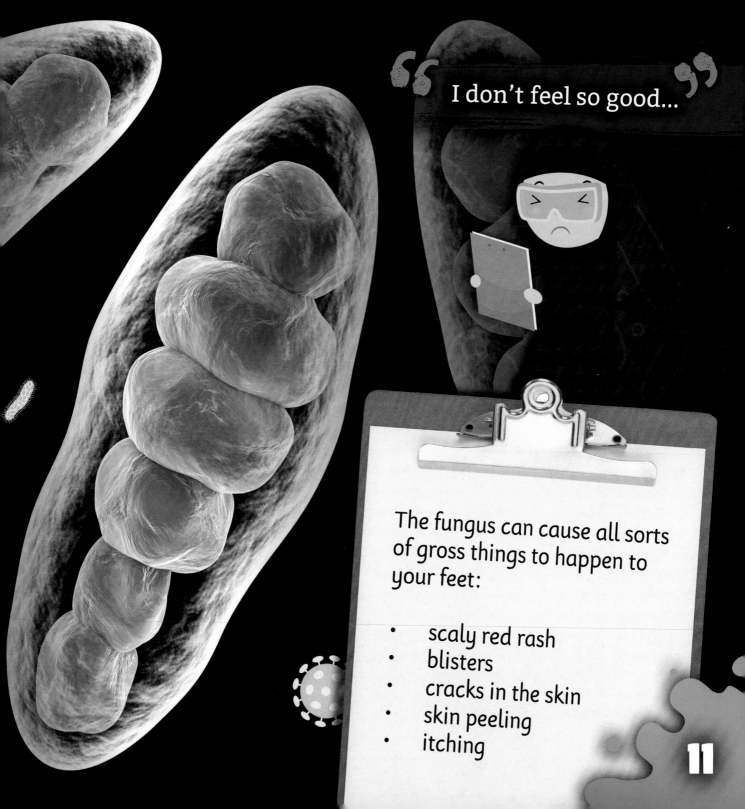

"I don't feel so good..."

The fungus can cause all sorts of gross things to happen to your feet:

- scaly red rash
- blisters
- cracks in the skin
- skin peeling
- itching

11

RINGWORM

Ringworm is caused by the same fungus that causes athlete's foot. The fungus can live anywhere on the body, such as the hair, skin, and nails.

Ringworm can spread from person to person. I'm making a "no hugging" rule.

Ringworm can cause lots of different things to happen to our bodies:

- ring-shaped red marks
- itching
- scaly skin
- spreading rash

It's called **ringworm**. It was never going to be good, was it?

ZOMBIE-ANT
FUNGUS

Other animals are <u>affected</u> by fungi too. There is a type of fungus that can turn ants into <u>zombies</u>.

Zombie ants?

Will somebody please get these fungi under control? "

The fungus takes over the ant's whole body and controls it. It makes the ant walk to a leaf or a branch, where the fungus can feed and grow.

"The fungus is coming out of the top of the ant's head!"

JOCK ITCH

Fungi can reach everywhere on the human body. EVERYWHERE. Jock itch is a fungal infection that can grow in your groin or between your bum cheeks.

"Fungi grow best in warm places on the body, which is why even your bum isn't safe."

Of all the fungal infections so far, this is the one I want least.

Jock itch can be found on your bottom and your thighs. It can cause:

- redness
- itching
- burning feelings
- rash
- dry, peeling skin

HONEY FUNGUS

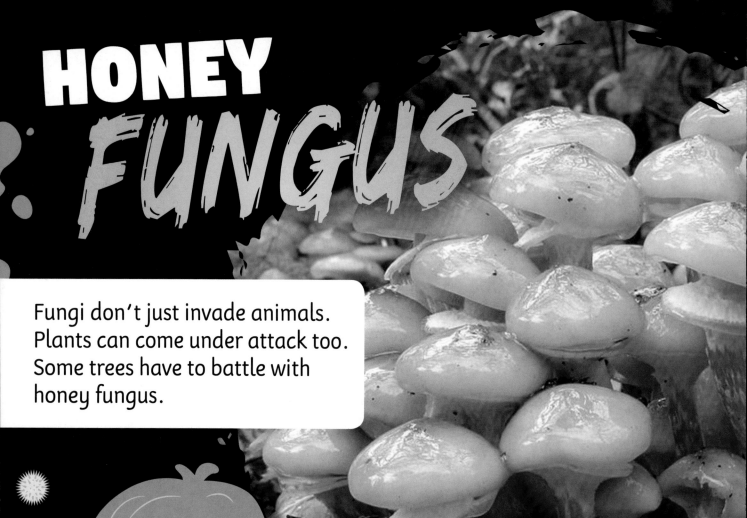

Fungi don't just invade animals. Plants can come under attack too. Some trees have to battle with honey fungus.

How can something sound so nice but be so **horrid?**

Honey fungus attacks the roots of a tree in order to kill it. It then feeds off the dead tree.

"Fungi are killing plants now? Won't somebody please save us?"

MOUTH THRUSH

A fungus called *Candida* is normally <u>harmless</u> to humans. However, it can cause an infection in your mouth called thrush.

"Harmless? Are you sure?"

CANDIDA

There has to be a way we can <u>treat</u> this...

Mouth thrush can be spotted quite easily. The fungus can cause:

- white spots
- cracks in the corners of the mouth
- things to taste differently
- pain and difficulty eating

21

FIGHTING BACK

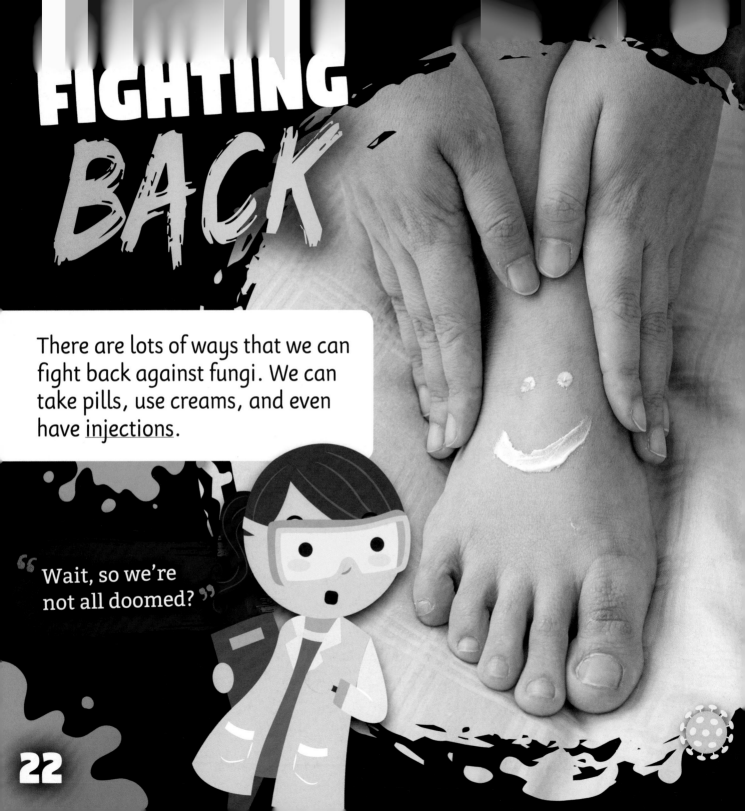

There are lots of ways that we can fight back against fungi. We can take pills, use creams, and even have <u>injections</u>.

"Wait, so we're not all doomed?"

Ha! Get back, fungi!

I've got cream, and I'm not afraid to use it!

Pills, creams, and injections can kill off the fungus or stop it from growing and getting bigger. The fight back against fungi has begun!

23

GLOSSARY

affect	to cause a change in something
harmless	not dangerous
infection	an illness caused by dirt or microbes getting into the body
injection	a measured amount of liquid medicine that is put into the body with a needle
invasion	when something comes into a place where it is not wanted or invited
microscope	a piece of scientific equipment that makes things look many times bigger
moist	slightly wet
poisonous	dangerous or deadly when eaten
spread	to move around from place to place to affect a larger area
treat	attempt to cure
zombie	a living thing that is controlled by something else

INDEX